Symbols, Landmarks, and Monuments

Ellis Island

Tamara L. Britton

ABDO Publishing Company

visit us at
www.abdopub.com

Published by ABDO Publishing Company, 4940 Viking Drive, Edina, Minnesota 55435.
Copyright © 2004 by Abdo Consulting Group, Inc. International copyrights reserved in all countries. No part of this book may be reproduced in any form without written permission from the publisher.

Printed in the United States.

Cover Photo: Corbis
Interior Photos: Corbis pp. 1, 5, 6-7, 8, 9, 12, 13, 14, 15, 16, 17, 18, 20, 22, 24, 25, 27, 28, 29; National Park Service p. 11

Series Coordinator: Kristin Van Cleaf
Editors: Kate A. Conley, Stephanie Hedlund
Art Direction & Maps: Neil Klinepier

Library of Congress Cataloging-in-Publication Data

Britton, Tamara L., 1963-
    Ellis Island / Tamara L. Britton.
        p. cm. -- (Symbols, landmarks, and monuments)
    Includes index.
    Summary: Explores the history of Ellis Island, which housed the United States' most important immigration processing center from 1892 through 1943, serving seventeen million immigrants.
    ISBN 1-59197-519-0
    1. Ellis Island Immigration Station (N.Y. and N.J.)--History--Juvenile literature. 2. United States--Emigration and immigration--History--Juvenile literature. [1. Ellis Island Immigration Station (N.Y. and N.J.) 2. United States--Emigration and immigration--History.] I. Title.

JV6484.B75 2004
304.8'73--dc22

                                                                2003057814

Contents

Ellis Island

Ellis Island is a small island in upper New York Harbor. Throughout U.S. history it has held a tavern, a fort, and a storage facility. Today, it is home to a museum.

In 1892, the island became the United States's most important center for processing **immigrants**. Over the next 60 years, 12 million immigrants passed through Ellis Island. They were seeking freedom and a better life in America.

In 1943, immigration processing moved away from the island. It soon became a **detainment** center and military facility. In 1954, the island closed. The buildings were **vandalized** and soon began to decay and fall into disrepair.

In time, people began to realize the importance of Ellis Island. A movement began to preserve this piece of history. After years of restoration, Ellis Island opened again. Today, people can visit the island and its museum.

The main building of Ellis Island

Fast Facts

√ Annie Moore, a 15-year-old girl from Ireland, was the first person to be registered at Ellis Island when it first opened on January 1, 1892. She was rushed inside and received a ten dollar gold coin.

√ Men usually immigrated first to find jobs and housing. Later they sent for their wives, children, and parents.

√ Immigrants often dressed up in their best traditional clothes in order to make a good impression on inspectors.

√ Ellis Island's busiest year was 1907. In a single day, 11,747 immigrants passed through Ellis Island. Nearly 200,000 were detained that year.

√ During its 50 years of operation, more than 3,500 immigrants died at Ellis Island, and more than 350 babies were born.

√ When Ellis Island was offered for sale, suggestions for rebuilding included an atomic research center, a casino, an amusement park, a women's prison, and "the perfect city of tomorrow."

√ During restoration, workers tested each of the 28,832 tiles on the Great Hall's high ceiling. Amazingly, only 17 tiles needed to be replaced!

√ Only some of Ellis Island's buildings have been restored. Organizations are currently raising money to restore the other buildings.

√ In 1998, the U.S. Supreme Court ruled that part of Ellis Island belongs to New Jersey. The island is only 1,300 feet (396 m) from the New Jersey shoreline.

Timeline

<u>1785</u>	√	Samuel Ellis tried to sell the island. New York bought it in 1807.
<u>1808</u>	√	The U.S. government bought Ellis Island from New York for $10,000.
<u>1813</u>	√	Ellis Island held Fort Gibson and housed large amounts of ammunition.
<u>1815-1860</u>	√	The first wave of immigrants from Europe to the United States occurred.
<u>1860-1890</u>	√	The second wave of immigration occurred.
<u>1890</u>	√	Ellis Island was selected as a site for a new immigration station.
<u>1890-1924</u>	√	The third wave of immigration occurred.
<u>1892</u>	√	The immigration station on Ellis Island opened on January 1.
<u>1897</u>	√	A fire destroyed the original wooden buildings on Ellis Island.
<u>1900</u>	√	The Ellis Island Immigration Center reopened.
<u>1943</u>	√	The island was used as a detainment center.
<u>1954</u>	√	Ellis Island officially closed and was offered for sale.
<u>1965</u>	√	Ellis Island became part of the National Park Service.
<u>1984</u>	√	Restoration of the main building began.
<u>1990</u>	√	Ellis Island Immigration Museum opened on September 10.
<u>1998</u>	√	The U.S. Supreme Court decided ownership of Ellis Island was to be split between New York and New Jersey.

Island in the Harbor

Ellis Island is one mile (1.6 km) southwest of Manhattan Island. It lies near Liberty Island, where the Statue of Liberty stands. Ellis Island was originally only about three acres (1 ha) in size. Today, it covers about 27 acres (11 ha).

Over the years, this little island has been known as Gull Island, Oyster Island, and many other names. By the late 1700s, Samuel Ellis had built a tavern on it. In 1807, the state of New York bought the island from his family.

New York Harbor in 1852

The next year, New York sold Ellis Island to the federal government. At that time, the government was worried about the possibility of war with Britain. So, it built Fort Gibson on the island to help protect the harbor.

In 1890, the government decided to build an **immigration** processing center on Ellis Island. They chose it because New York was a main point of entry for immigrants. An island would also isolate the immigrants until they were inspected.

Before Ellis Island

Small- to medium-scale immigration to the United States started with the colonies in the early 1600s and lasted through the 1700s. Then in the 1800s, waves of immigrants began flooding into America. Immigrants landed in different areas of the country, but many came through New York. In 1855, this state created one of the first immigration stations, called Castle Garden. But the facility was too small. And, immigrants were often cheated when they exchanged their money as well as other ways. So, the federal government took over and decided to build a station at Ellis Island.

Immigrants arrive at Castle Garden.

Building the Center

Ellis Island was too small for the construction. To make more space, workers enlarged it with **landfill**. Construction began on the building in 1891.

Ellis Island officially opened on January 1, 1892. Unfortunately, the building had been constructed mostly of wood. In June 1897, a fire burned it to the ground.

New plans were soon underway. This time, the building would be made of brick and steel. Workers added more landfill to further enlarge the island. The main building, power house, and laundry opened in 1900.

Immigrants entered on the first floor of the main building, where they could store their luggage. Then, they climbed stairs to the second floor.

Around the outside of this floor were rooms for medical exams. In the middle was the registry room, which was also called the Great Hall. There, inspectors held the legal exams.

More space was soon needed. The island was expanded with **landfill** for a third time. In 1902, a hospital was built. Two years later, a railroad ticket office, dining room, and third floor were added. Soon, dormitories and a second hospital were also completed.

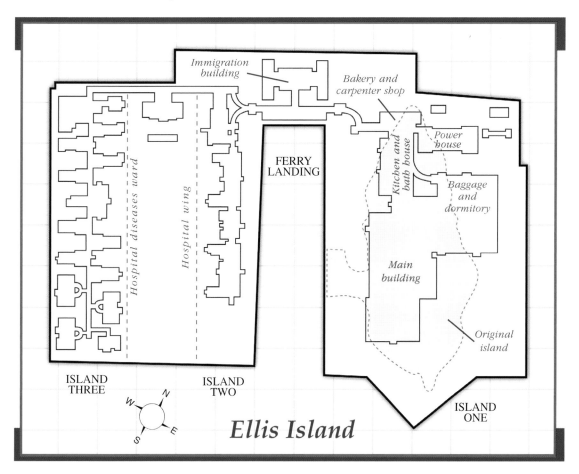

Immigration building

Bakery and carpenter shop

Power house

Kitchen and bath house

Baggage and dormitory

FERRY LANDING

Hospital diseases ward

Hospital wing

Main building

Original island

ISLAND THREE

ISLAND TWO

ISLAND ONE

N W E S

Ellis Island

The Long Journey

Many reasons brought millions of people from Europe to the United States. Often, **immigrants** fled governments that were led by **dictators** or **communists**. In some countries there was not enough land, and people were starving. Many also suffered from religious **persecution**.

Many of these people had heard about the freedom that people enjoyed in America. The United States offered jobs, freedom of speech and religion, and the opportunity to own land. The government was a **democracy**. And if people worked hard, they could be anything they wanted to be.

Companies often used posters, such as this one, to advertise their ships.

For these reasons, people left for America, hoping for a better life. Between 1824 and 1924, almost 34 million people **immigrated** to the United States. Most arrived between 1890 and 1924. Nearly 80 percent entered through Ellis Island.

Ship passengers crowd on deck to see the Statue of Liberty.

Immigrants crowd together in steerage.

In the late 1800s and early 1900s, most **immigrants** arrived from Europe by steamship. Most immigrants could not afford to buy first- or even second-class tickets for the journey to America. However, ships offered a less expensive passage called steerage.

Steerage was located in the lower decks of a ship. There, metal bunk beds were crowded into small cabins. Many people occupied a small space.

In steerage, passengers did not have many opportunities to take baths. In addition, the air was stuffy and smelled bad. Steerage passengers did not receive the best food. They ate prunes, fish, potatoes, soup, and low-quality meat.

These trying conditions made the two-week trip across the Atlantic Ocean long and difficult. But when the ship reached New York, **immigrants** knew their journey was almost over. They crowded onto the deck to see Manhattan. The Statue of Liberty welcomed them to the land of opportunity.

Immigrants wait to come ashore after reaching the United States.

On the Island

When ships entered New York Harbor, they first stopped at a **quarantine** station on the Hudson River. There, officials inspected the first- and second-class passengers. If found acceptable, these passengers entered the country right off the ship.

During peak years, millions of immigrants flooded Ellis Island, causing a long wait and crowded conditions.

After docking, steerage passengers received a tag with the number of the ship's **manifest** they were recorded on. The **immigrants** then boarded **ferries** for the trip to Ellis Island. After leaving their bags in the baggage room, the immigrants were ready for inspection.

In the 1900s, social service agencies complained about the waves of **immigrants**. They said that the number of immigrants seeking public assistance made it difficult to provide for everyone.

For this reason, officials decided not to admit people who could not support themselves into the country. As a result, people were subject to many tests before they were allowed into the United States.

Women were not allowed to enter the country unless their husband or a male relative accompanied them.

Doctors started examining the **immigrants** from the minute they stepped off the **ferries**. As people climbed the stairs to the second floor, doctors watched for more than 50 symptoms of illness. They looked closely for signs of cholera, tuberculosis, mental illness, and trachoma.

Inspectors check immigrants for trachoma, a disease that could cause blindness.

If an **immigrant** appeared sick, a doctor marked a letter on his or her coat with chalk. The letter indicated the suspected problem. Marked immigrants moved to medical **quarantine** for further examination. Healthy immigrants were allowed to move on to the legal exam.

Legal inspectors, working with interpreters, asked the immigrants many questions. They verified the information that the immigrant had recorded on the ship's **manifest**. They asked questions such as the person's name and occupation, and whether he or she was married.

Immigrants had to prove that they could work, and that they could get a job. The immigrants had to show inspectors their money. They needed to be able to support themselves until they found a job.

Immigrants that did not pass the tests would be **deported** to their home countries. The shipping company that brought the person to America had to pay for the return ticket. Officials hoped this would make the shipping companies careful to bring only immigrants who could pass.

Immigrants waiting for their inquiries eat together in Ellis Island's dining hall.

Inspectors wanted to make sure **immigrants** had the best chance of succeeding in America. About 20 percent of immigrants did not pass inspection and were sent to Special Inquiry. About four out of five people who were sent to inquiry eventually passed.

Immigrants that passed received a landing card. It was their ticket to a new life. People who received the card were free to go.

Before starting their journey, they traded their foreign money for U.S. dollars at the money exchange. Then, those who still had farther to travel bought train tickets. Immigrants with relatives in New York City had joyous reunions at the **ferry** landing. They had finally arrived in America.

Staying on Ellis Island

Ellis Island eventually had a kitchen, dining hall, dormitory, laundry, and hospital. These areas housed and fed the immigrants who didn't immediately pass the health or legal inspections.

Those who were sick but would recover stayed in the island's hospital. Others were held for further testing or questioning. Immigrants could stay on the island for a few days up to a few weeks. Those who didn't pass were deported, but they could appeal to the Board of Special Inquiry. Immigrants were deported for reasons such as mental or physical illness, poor physical condition, or political beliefs.

Changing Times

Waves of **immigrants** continued to arrive in America. In the early 1900s, millions of immigrants passed through an overcrowded Ellis Island. The wave hit its peak in 1907, when 11,747 people passed through in one day.

In 1914, **World War I** started in Europe. The United States entered the fighting in 1917. By then, the oceans were not safe for shipping. As a result, immigration nearly stopped during the war. When it ended, immigrants began coming once again.

Immigrants often worked for low wages in factories.

But the experience of **immigrants** in America had changed. As early as the 1800s, some Americans had been suspicious of immigrants. **World War I** caused people to become even more distrustful.

Some Americans began to view immigrants as poor, diseased criminals who took jobs away from American citizens. In response, lawmakers began to pass anti-immigration laws.

In 1921, President Warren G. Harding passed the first **quota** act. This law restricted immigrants by nationality. Officials looked at the 1910 **census** to determine how many immigrants from each country were living in the United States. The quota act allowed only 3 percent of that number to enter the country in one year.

In 1924, the National Origins Act lowered that figure to 2 percent. In addition, it used the 1890 census as a guide. That year, there were fewer immigrants from each country in America. So, even fewer people could enter than before.

In the early 1930s, America was suffering through the Great Depression. Jobs were scarce, and some Americans thought that **immigrants** were taking what few jobs there were.

For this reason, officials began to **deport** people who could not prove they came to the country legally. Other immigrants left, discouraged by the poor **economy**. In 1932, more people left the country than immigrated into it.

By the late 1930s, Ellis Island was almost empty. In 1939, the beginning of **World War II** increased the flow of immigrants from Europe. But as time went on, fewer and fewer people came through Ellis Island.

The United States joined World War II in 1941. The government **detained** Japanese, Germans, and Italians on the island in 1943. The Coast Guard used some of the island's buildings for storage. In the 1950s, suspected **communists** and fascists stayed there while under investigation.

In 1954, a new law passed. It said people under investigation were allowed to be paroled until their hearing. Now, **detained immigrants** did not have to stay on Ellis Island until they met with government officials. The law also closed Ellis Island on November 19 of that year.

Ellis Island stands nearly empty on November 8, 1954, just before being shut down.

Preserving the Past

In the 1950s, people developed many plans for Ellis Island. However, when the federal government put the island up for sale, nobody offered enough money for it. The buildings stood empty. They began to deteriorate and were damaged by **vandals** and looters.

In 1965, President Lyndon B. Johnson made Ellis Island part of the Statue of Liberty National Monument. This made the island part of the National Park Service. But it remained neglected. In 1976, the island's main building opened for tours, but it closed again in 1984.

The Statue of Liberty-Ellis Island Foundation was created in 1982. The group raised money to restore the island. The members wanted the buildings to look as they did between 1918 and 1924. That was when many of the **immigrants** had passed through.

By 1984, the Statue of Liberty-Ellis Island Foundation had raised enough money to begin work. It took almost two years to dry the rooms of the seawater that had soaked into them. The inside and outside of the buildings were repaired. The restoration took eight years and cost nearly $160 million.

Ellis Island's buildings began to decay after standing empty for many years.

Ellis Island Today

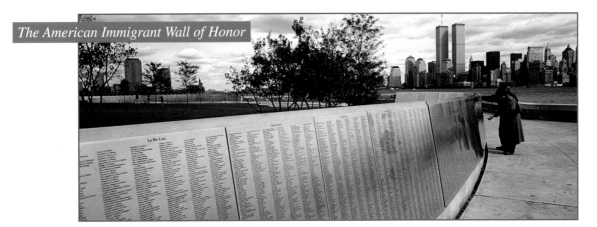

The American Immigrant Wall of Honor

About 100 million Americans have an ancestor who **immigrated** through Ellis Island. These immigrants wrote to friends and relatives in their home countries. They described their journey from Ellis Island into the land of opportunity.

The Ellis Island Immigration Museum opened in 1990. Today, people once again take the **ferry** to Ellis Island. They go to see the beautifully restored buildings. They imagine how their relatives felt as they passed through the island.

In the Great Hall, the Ellis Island **Immigration** Museum has many exhibits. Visitors can see items brought from other countries by immigrants. They can read firsthand accounts of what it was like to immigrate.

The museum's American Immigrant Wall of Honor has 420,000 immigrants' names carved on it. It honors the millions who once came through this island on their way to a better life. Ellis Island is a **landmark** that reminds many Americans where they come from, and why.

Today the Great Hall has been restored and is part of the museum.

Glossary

census - a count of the population of a country or area.

communism - a social and economic system in which everything is owned by the government and is distributed to the people as needed.

democracy - a governmental system in which the people vote on how to run their country.

deport - to force someone who is not a citizen to leave the country.

detainment - a period of being held in custody while waiting for a trial or hearing.

dictator - a ruler with complete control, who usually governs in a cruel or unfair way.

economy - the way a nation uses its money, goods, and natural resources.

ferry - a boat used to carry people, goods, and vehicles across a body of water.

immigration - entry into another country to live. A person who immigrates is called an immigrant.

landfill - garbage layered with earth. It is used to build up an area of land.

landmark - an important structure of historical or physical interest.

manifest - a ship's list of passengers or cargo.

persecution - harassment due to one's origin, religion, or other beliefs.

quarantine - when people suspected of having a disease are separated from others in order to stop the disease from spreading.

quota - a limit to the number of people allowed to immigrate in a year.

vandalize - intentional damage done to public or private property. People who do this are called vandals.

World War I - from 1914 to 1918, fought in Europe. The United States, Great Britain, France, Russia, and their allies were on one side. Germany, Austria-Hungary, and their allies were on the other side.

World War II - from 1939 to 1945, fought in Europe, Asia, and Africa. The United States, France, Great Britain, the Soviet Union, and their allies were on one side. Germany, Italy, Japan, and their allies were on the other side.

Web Sites

To learn more about Ellis Island, visit ABDO Publishing Company on the World Wide Web at **www.abdopub.com**. Web sites about the island are featured on our Book Links page. These links are routinely monitored and updated to provide the most current information available.

Index